NORTHERN VOICES 2001

poetry Pt today

NORTHERN VOICES 2001

Edited by Suzy Walton

First published in Great Britain in 2001 by Poetry
Today, an imprint of
Penhaligon Page Ltd, Remus House, Coltsfoot Drive,
Woodston, Peterborough. PE2 9JX

© Copyright Contributors 2000

All rights reserved. No part of this publication may be
reproduced, stored in a retrieval system, or transmitted
in any form or by any means, without prior permission
from the author(s).

A Catalogue record for this book is available from the
British Library

ISBN 1 86226 641 7

Typesetting and layout, Penhaligon Page Ltd, England.
Printed and bound by Forward Press Ltd, England

Foreword

Northern Voices 2001 is a compilation of poetry, featuring some of our finest poets. This book gives an insight into the essence of modern living and deals with the reality of life today. We think we have created an anthology with a universal appeal.

There are many technical aspects to the writing of poetry and *Northern Voices 2001* contains free verse and examples of more structured work from a wealth of talented poets.

Poetry is a coat of many colours. Today's poets write in a limitless array of styles: traditional rhyming poetry is as alive and kicking today as modern free verse. Language ranges from easily accessible to intricate and elusive.

Poems have a lot to offer in our fast-paced 'instant' world. Reading poems gives us an opportunity to sit back and explore ourselves and the world around us.

Contents

My Girls	Barry Richardson	1
Memoirs Of Sweet Billie	P Brewer	2
Childhood Lovers	Amanda Carroll	4
The Rain	Sarah Feeney	5
Sitting	Gill Kendall	6
May Magic	Marie Knowles	7
Snowdrops	Angela Pritchard	8
Our Ken	Brenda M Lawrenson	9
Blue Glass On A Grey Day	Elizabeth Thorpe	10
Cupboard Love	Vivien Holden	11
Melancholy	John Sanderson	12
Whitehead Gardens, Tottington	John H Hope	13
English Winter	Marjorie Piggins	14
Peace	Anne Wareing	15
Midnight Drive	Julie Ashpool	16
Old King Mangle	Terry Coneys	17
Nature's Way	Eleanor Haydon Sanderson	18
Universal Denial	Christine A Smithies	19
A Metre Of Earth!	Mollie Wade	20
Madame Butterfly	Amanda Beattie	21
Tee For Two	John Kirkham	22
Lonely	Angela Carter	23
Dear Friends	Susie Hughes	24
My Little Boy Bob	Maurice Penk	25
Renovations	Anne Bland	26
Houndbound	Marilyn Campbell	27
This Is 'My' River	Joseph Williams	28
The Seasons Are Always Changing	Brenda Russell	30
Roy Remembered	Brian Hartley	32
Carer's Lament	Patricia Bowe	33
They're Going Shopping	April Treddle	34
Thinking	Dorothy Knight	36
Shattered Dreams	Dorothy Morris-Hague	37
Another Space	Susie J Burnette	38
Life	Elizabeth Spencer	39

The Nursery School Teacher	Joan Kelly	40
Prophet Mohammed	Haji Masud Ahmed	41
The Silent Army	Jean Wood	42
Strange Encounter	Edith M Stott	43
Michael's Poem	Joan Latham-Trotzko	44
The Searching Eye	Joan Thompson	45
St Crispin's Day	Brian Acton	46
Autumn Leaves	Ethel M Crowther	48
Winter's Approach	Peggy Norton	49
Flowers Of The Wilderness	Edna W Mills	50
The Same Sky	Jean Jackson	51
The Dreamer	Abigail E Jones	52
Venus	Nicola Avino	53
The Market Hall	Gordon Harper	54
Compact	Dean Urquhart	55
Not For Him	Brenda Gill	56
Loving Children	James S Cameron	57
Fled Is That Music	Jason Redvers Latham	58
If Only I Could Fly	Winifred Wardle	59
Neither A Duck Or A Swan	Stephen Hibbeler	60
Flying	Cinsia Wilde	61
Autumn Glory	Alan Hattersley	62
E Tenebris Lux	Janet Cavill	63
Time Is Precious	M Rossi	64
Beauty ~ Louise	Pettr Manson-Herrod	65
Autumn Signs	Linda Bellamy	66
Heart Strings	Alan Gale	67
A Moment For Life	Rachel C Zaino	68
My Italian Hat	Sandra Oates	69
The Swan	A Jones	70
Game Of Chance	Candice Buchanan	71
Mother Nature	D Williams	72
Ode To The Braying Donkeys	John Morrison	73
The Good Old Days	Peggy Hunter	74
Have You Been There?	Catherine O'Neill	75
Untitled	Nan Milton	76
My Memory	Betty Park	77
Laura	H Muir	78

The Old House	Annie McKimmie	79
The Rain	Mary Hudson	80
Hope	William D Watt	81
Brigadoon	Norman Bissett	82
Scotland My Home	Hazel Smith	83
Bonnie Dundee	Jean Hendrie	84
The Home Help's Holy Grail	Alan Pow	85
Kitty	Lynsey Calderwood	86
McLeod In The Clouds	John Carrey	87
Eternal Youth	Kathleen Dow	88
A Day	Gillian Hare-Scott	89
Sunshine	Denis M Rae	90
Big Issue	Byde	91
Before The Concrete	John Bonnar	92
from: Nursery Rhymes	Jonathan Claxton	94
Castletown Carol	Elizabeth Stephens	95
Pie Crust and Pot Noodle	Val Stephenson	96
What Is The Meaning Of Life?	Kathryn Kaupa	97
The Fog On The Tyne	Norman H McGlasham	98
Ladies Of The Skies	Donald John Tye	99
Dream Catcher	Barry Cuda	100
Paper	Walter Christmas	101
A Thought For Winter	Vivian Finlay	102
The Key	Kathleen Potter	103

My Girls

I'll sit and watch
My young girls at play
How bright their minds
How sharp their ways
For all too soon
Their childhood gone
And womanhood
Will bloom along
From little girls
To young maids fair
Who will they meet
When, why, and where
And what becomes
Of dear old dad
Will I become
A dear grandad
But that's the future
Far away
For now I'll sit
And watch them play

Barry Richardson

Memoirs of Sweet Billie

There was my dog to write I must
To tell you she was soft to touch
She my friend a faithful friend
Always with me right to the end

Her name was Billie, Billie sweet
Everyone loved her when we meet
So gentle, loving and given
Billie her name now in heaven

She's black and brown with hazel eyes
Floppy ears coat so fine
She's sloppy and cuddly with a cute little snout
So Mona Lisa eat your heart out

She follows me around from morning to night
A lost lamb but that was alright
When she hungry, she would pick up her dish
Feed me Feed me that was her wish

Her favourite food was chocolate smartee
She could eat them from morning to tea
Milk was a must because she drunk plenty
The milkman has to collect many empties

When we go on our walkabouts
Sometime she gets lost but hear me shout
Billie where are you I give you ten
She knew ten seconds or something then

The only problem could be found
She loved to chase bunnies on the ground
Then chasing them to their underground
She loses me deep in the wood deep down

Her punishment is a lead for a while
It's better than a smacking or getting me riled
Because if she got lost I miss Billie so mild
As it take away my smiles

Her love for a ride in the car
She knew peep peep and tat tar
Peep peep meant car, tat tar meant walk
Where are we going, if only she could talk

So my story end about sweet Billie
I put it into one, she was silly
She used to rolled upright to rub her belly
So her nickname was a silly Billie

Now she have gone to a great place in the sky
But her memories live on with tears in my eyes
Blue bill wood Billie mountain to name but a few
Billie sweet Billie I do miss you

P Brewer

Childhood Lovers

Charlie spies Suzie
Across the square
Suzie glances back
Together they stare

They ran to each other
Remembering back to their childhood days
Playing in the sunshine
Before they went their own ways

Suzie had cried
Charlie had screamed
To see each other no more
Except when they dreamed

Charlie had cried
Charlie was sad
Was it a punishment
Had he been bad

Suzie had sobbed
Suzie had wept
She was so unhappy
Except when she slept

Charlie clutched Suzie's hand
Went down on one knee
'I've waited so long
Will you marry me?'

Amanda Carroll

The Rain

The rain, oh the rain
It patters on my windows
And it crashes on the floor
and it drips and it drops
on my door, door, door

   Sarah Feeney (7)

Sitting

Sitting in the tent all alone
No one to talk to
No one at all
Oh what peace surrounds me
The birds chirping and the sheep bleating
This is my heaven even only for a short while
Before I need to go back to work and home once more
Is this life I live hell I do not know
But when my time comes and I go to heaven
Please leave me in my tent sat alone
Listening to the birds and distant sheep bleating
Watching the fells and all pass by.

Gill Kendall

May Magic

First the blossoms pink and white
Dazzle us with colour bright,
Next the hawthorns' shower of flowers
Splash the meadows with white bowers,
The rhododendrons' colours blaze
Kissed by the sunshine's dappled rays
Daisies Bluebells Buttercups
Reside in hedgerows, fields and woods
And flowers scent the evening air
We take more time to stand and stare
At all the wonder that is spring
Awed by the beauty that it brings

Marie Knowles

Snowdrops

Planted with love in the autumn,
Buried beneath a mound,
Unseen at the start of winter,
Snowdrops sleep in the ground.

As winter days start to lengthen,
Tiny bulbs start to grow,
There's such joy when you discover
Green shoots starting to show.

A few cold, sunny days follow,
White speckles among the green,
You examine them more closely,
Flowers can now be seen.

White heads dancing in the breezes
Just to let us all know,
Promising brighter spring mornings,
Putting on quite a show.

Winter will soon be behind us,
Herald of spring is here,
Seasons have now turned full circle,
Welcome to this new year.

Angela Pritchard

Our Ken

Across the dappled meadow, untrod upon by men,
    Through the daisies and the lush green grass, I can see our Ken.
Four dogs bouncing round him, green wellies all a'gleam.
    Ken is in his heaven, it's not a passing dream.
Big Sheba's chasing Oliver, my Lass and Badge a'dance.
    He loves them, they love him,
With every single glance.
    But with the coming evening sun,
They wander off, and still,
    We mourn, we grieve, we miss him,
And we always will.

    Brenda M Lawrenson (Ebor)

Blue Glass On A Grey Day

Sitting alone
In this gallery cafe
On this grey
Manchester morning
It caught my eye
On the waitress's tray
Without any warning
Just a small blue bottle
But to me a bit of magic
It caught the light
And I knew I had to have it
She looked at me in surprise
When I pointed out its beauty
She offered it to me
With such a smile
Before she went off duty
So here I sit at my table
Still life with blue bottle

Elizabeth Thorpe

Cupboard Love

My cat loves me very much
It's plain for all to see
He rubs his head around my legs
And looks at me so lovingly

He follows me around the house
Even up the stairs
Keeping me within his sight
I know he really cares

Now he's purring oh so loud
And jumping on my knee
With pounding paws and sharpest claws
I wonder what he's telling me

What really is his motive
For this pretentious mood
Who does he think he's fooling
It's clear he's after food

I lovingly put down his meal
His ardour seems to pass
For, after food, where has he gone . . .
Out sleeping in the longest grass

He doesn't want to know me now
Of this I have the proof
I'm being ignored and what is more
His manner now is quite aloof

Ah well he's still my little friend
Despite his daily ploy
I wouldn't be without my cat
His presence gives me so much joy

Vivien Holden

Melancholy

Lonely as the floating leaf
At the mercy of the wind
No roots nor sense of purpose
Good Lord how I must have sinned

The sun is shining brightly
Yet my sky is void and black
Drifting through the wilderness
In which all directions lack

The wind has changed direction
And is blowing very cold
Oh God, for some affection
For a helping hand to hold

I can't see the stars at night
Or bright colours by the day
Although I have my eyesight
I feel blind in a strange way

No man should be an island
Or be lonely in a crowd
No person who is living
Should be attired in a shroud

If love makes the world go round
Then spread it with every haste
A man whose world is loveless
Is a certain tragic waste

Give me a soul to turn to
Give me a song to sing
Give me a love to cling to
Then I'd have everything

    John Sanderson

Whitehead Gardens, Tottington

In time
they'll probably put houses there.
Not terra cotta Accrington and slatey grey,
more likely rough-cut cheese-blocks thinly stitched
like those grey veterans sand-blasted in rain.

As it is,
you perch meccano-rigid on a backless bench,
admire the council-clipped lawn patches and the stream
wriggling, giggling from a culvert somewhere underneath,
cutting a bed through crowded shrubberies.

You'll usually be alone,
maybe the odd stray mongrel, watching, resentful,
cocking its leg against a silver birch,
and there's unease between you
and traffic grumblings just behind
coming at you from a future dream.

Could be
the vandalised stone terrace at the far end,
paving smashed, fist-shattered teeth,
or maybe the dedication tablet on the wall
and seven pale ghosts keening in the trees.

Close down; be still.
If you listen through the inner ear
half-a-century peels back the traffic-rush of now,
And from a Christmas night-sky drops
the mad corporal's vindictive hammer
exploding smoke-stone cottages in spite
and shattering a church's brittle saints
out of time.

John H Hope

English Winter

Old red roofs above old stone walls ~
    Scarlet hips as Winter falls ~
Shining white clouds high over all ~
    Late rosy apples nodding on the garden wall.

Winter-flowering plants galore:
    Jasmine, aconite and hellebore;
Snowdrops, Winter pansies,
    And half a hundred more.

Bluetits, greenfinches, robin redbreast
    Flit about with joy and zest ~
Green woodpeckers, waxwings and little goldcrest ~
    Pink jays and stockdoves with purple vest.

When people say England's Winter's grey
    I shake with rage, just like a jelly!
They're all so blind ~ our Winters grey?
    Ye gods! Not on your nelly!

Marjorie Piggins

Peace

A rocking horse, all forlorn
In an empty room
Thinks of children's laughter
Absent now, there's only gloom

They're grown now and gone
Out into adult worlds
Leaving childish fantasies
Along with childish curls

No longer do they fight and fuss
Nor pull the horse's mane
No longer scratch with spurs
Its sides in racing game

Faded now, its saddle torn
From each roughly ridden mile
The rocking horse stood very still
And allowed itself a smile!

Anne Wareing

Midnight Drive

When the hardness sets inside
frigid memory of a red hot anger,
burning the flicker it sets alight
in recall of steadiness, memory forgets.

I cry new temper, meant to keep its
long lost, close cold cool;
chilling hot it fixes gaze, awakes
the warmth of kindness, but lasts
only a minute.

I had awoken on the hard shoulder.
Froze inside like those around
and saw the blood red pulling
the steering wheel away from me.

Jazz sings mellow on the radio;
beckons me to its bellowing side: it touches
that deeper than diamonds of the soul;
I forget those words when this is so.

I pull away and sleep at the wheel;
wait for the anger to slowly heal, forever
keeping my cool.

It was meant to be bliss, this
freedom in a car, away from words.
But I saw the red and wove
down streets paved with ice
black and dreamy, with no place to go.

Julie Ashpool

Old King Mangle

King of the washdays I used to be,
Every Monday I would oversee,
My dolly tubs and dolly blue,
Gas boilers, possers, and scrubbing board too.

My rollers grinding the water away,
Clouds of steam from the boiler all day,
Washing lines full, wash pegged and flying,
The sun's warm rays helped with the drying.

For many years I reigned supreme,
Till one day there came a washing machine,
They wheeled me out onto the lawn,
A garden ornament, quite forlorn.

But machines come and go. I'm still to be seen,
I know I've been granted a pardon.
I mean what can you do with an old washing machine?
You can't put that in the garden.

So here I stand amidst the flowers,
Exposed to the weather and drenched by the showers,
Painted and varnished, chains full of oil,
Now I'm King of the garden. Reprieved from my toil.

Terry Coneys

Nature's Way

Of the writing of books there is no end,
As in creative art and upon lovely music we ever depend,
Inspiring sounds of song, life's joy these blessings bring
Akin to pretty poetry, the bluebird sings merrily on wing.
Our dear feathered friends build their nest in sunny spring,
Perfected in detail, each precious leaf on tree and flower,
Sweet scented stock and yellow daffodil grow tall in April's shower,
Whilst red and gold butterfly glow with prideful power,
In field the newly born lamb frolics freely in summer's air,
Busy bees making honey, their wisdom supremely rare.
Robin redbreast returns as winter's season draws nigh,
Unique shapes of white snowflake softly fall neath a misty sky,
Autumn's tree sheds its worn leaves, soon tis so bare,
Until again they'll grow strong with God's tender love and care,
These wonders of nature surround us year by year,
Regardless of passing time, through the ageless process of prayer.

Eleanor Haydon Sanderson

Universal Denial
(Dedicated to all who live on Langley Estate, Middleton)

We are the forgotten people
Driven by forces we do not control,
Fighting a system for survival
But strength comes when all is lost.
Where I live Hope ebbs and flows
The blood of the young carelessly spilt
Street life is charged with electric anger
Come down from your towers
And face the mirror you refuse to look at
This place where I live it's not as far as Mars,
But we are aliens an experimental tennis ball
While our own kind walk around in suits
Parading government power.
Where were they when the children starved
To whom do their loyalties belong
Who is responsible for our homes
The Rochdaliens or who, tell me!
Who will rebuild our town our culture
We are being sold off like slaves
Was not slavery abolished?
Hope is eternally bound up in our children
Shall we also sell our children.

Christine A Smithies

A Metre Of Earth!

The slugs slide round the garden
Nibbling at the plants
They slip beneath the pathside stones
Disturbing little ants.
The ants go scurrying to and fro
Their work is not disrupted.
A passing thrush espies the action
His flight is interrupted!
A snail in curly spotted shell
Hides beneath a bush
She does not want to be the lunch
Of a sharp-eyed mistle thrush.
The thrush is very chary
Of the tabby cat who's sleeping.
(If he fluttered any closer
He would see a slit eye peeping).
The butterflies of various hues
Are buddleia decorating.

The peace in Nature's garden
Is very enervating!

Mollie Wade

Madame Butterfly

Her world is a library full of mystery and madness,
disaster, success, laughter and sadness.

She's the life of the party, they all know her name.
They don't know her secrets, they don't know her game!

They had no reason to do what they did,
no one knows of it, she's kept it well hid.

She'd take a beating from this one and that,
then she'd put on a smile and pick up her hat,

Move on to the next leaf and give it a try,
just carrying on, never asking why.

Abuse and assault she's taken it all,
they keep knocking her down, but she still stands up tall.

Getting on with her world, she's absorbed in her life,
She keeps her balance as she walks the knife

While a Caterpillar crawls from leaf to leaf,
It looks out for itself and deals with grief.

Then things get too much, it can't cope with the day,
It gives up its fight and hides away

Has it gone crazy? Or will it just die?
or has it just turned into ~ *a Butterfly?*

Flies away from the world, mile after mile.
Never looks back, just keeps going and *smiles!*

Amanda Beattie

Tee For Two

He stood on the tee and put his ball upon a peg.
Took his stance, checked his grip and slightly bent his leg.
When all appeared in order and everything taught seemed there,
He swung the club with all his might and hit nothing but fresh
                                                                                air.
That is one, his partner said, as if he didn't know.
So again he set himself to have another go.
This time, he was more successful and actually hit the ball,
But twenty feet was the total distance, that it managed to roll.
A downhill lie, behind the ladies tee, didn't look so good,
So he made the decision of not to play a wood.
An iron shot is what I need so as not to be over ambitious,
But everything went wrong again because his swing was much to
                                                                                vicious.
He hit the ground behind the ball and took a great big divot
But the ball remained where it was, as he continued with his pivot.
The next four strokes he played quite well, but not quite good
                                                                                enough,
For there were still two hundred yards to go and he was in the rough.
Thrice more the sun it glinted on his flailing wedge,
Until the ball went forward and finished in a hedge.
An unplayable lie, I can drop for one, according to the rule,
He told his playing partner, not wanting to appear a fool,
Arm out straight, shoulder high and drop within one club's length,
The ball sat up quite nicely, so he hit it with all his strength.
His chosen four iron, hit the ball, as good as good can be,
But then it bounced quite badly and rolled behind a tree,
A sideways chip, a little pitch and the ball was in the sand,
Two missed shots with his sand-iron then it came out grand.
Three putts later and the ball was in the hole, and
He felt quite elated as he achieved his goal.
I'm not quite sure how many said he, because I've taken plenty,
I hope you do better on the second hole, because you
Were down in twenty!

John Kirkham

Lonely

I'm sitting here all on my own
and feeling so low
no one to talk to and
nowhere to go.

I stare out of my window
and watch people pass me by.
I notice the birds in my
garden taking the bread I
put out for them and fly.

I turn the radio on so
to hear someone's voice other
than my own.
The music they played
brought back memories of
when I wasn't so alone.

You left this world so suddenly
leaving me on my own.
I know I'm being selfish by sitting here
and having this little moan.
I pray the Lord will take me
when the time is right
so until then my love sleep tight and goodnight.

Angela Carter

Dear Friends

As the day of departure draws nearer and I have to leave,
I feel as if my heart will break.
The tears well up inside me. I sob. I ache.
I observe every feature of your face, to me now so dear,
As if to capture the image of you forever in my mind.
I want to hold on tight to you, to all the happy memories,
The conversations, the coffees and the caring, which we have shared.
I want to hold you in my heart, forever near.
We hug each other close and the world stops still,
For a brief moment the pain of departure is postponed.
As my life is slowly dismantled and packed away in boxes,
I wish there was another way,
A way I didn't have to say 'Goodbye.'

Susie Hughes

My Little Boy Bob

Please listen to these words, as they unfold
They will tell you about my little boy Bob
Who had a little heart of gold
When Bob was born I smiled with glee
To think little boy Bob belonged to me
But as we got home from school one day
Little boy Bob went out to play
It was then this driver hit the kerb
And a drunken driver had to swerve
It was then this drunk hit my little boy Bob
So off to hospital they took him there
My little boy Bob went into intensive care
So I knelt and prayed to God
I asked Him not to take my little boy Bob
But God took Bob it was His will
But in my heart little boy Bob liveth still
So would-be drink drivers please be told
Don't drink and drive and take
Another little heart of gold

Maurice Penk

Renovations

What's all the fuss?
All this coming and going
The painting ~ the plumbing
The hammering and sawing
Such a to-do to keep the house right
I knew that darned shelf
Would collapse in the night!
Never to worry, just go on paying
For new fence in the field
And getting the hay in
For carpets and curtains and new settee too
All got to be new ~ just any won't do.
Who's going to worry after your day?
'She kept it quite nice'
The locals will say.
So passes on to the next generation
The young ones come on
With their new creations.
It looks very tidy and clean all in all
The chair in the corner
The lights on the wall
One's ever so grateful
To people who care
Who keep the old homestead
In first rate repair.

Anne Bland

Housebound

How frustrating you may say
To sit and while the hours away
To contemplate the world outside
They cannot know the hours I've cried

I've watched them come, I watch them go
Some just wave those I know
From my window I survey
Friendly faces day by day

Some pass by and simply stare
Why am I just sitting there
How I wish that I could go
Out with those I do not know

To walk, skip, jump and run
Share the joy, feel the sun
Alas my world is in this chair
Useless body once so fair

Trapped am I a crippled cell
Perhaps forever who can tell
What miracle may be my fate?
So here I sit and always wait.

Marilyn Campbell

This Is 'My' River
(The Ribble)

From the steep boggy side of Dod Fell Hill
From God's earth as cam and Gayle Becks I spill
And over the lush mossy banks of Cam Fell
The birth and journey of a great river I will tell
As on I flow betwixt Ingleborough and Pen-Y-Ghent
Through many pretty villages my infant waters are sent
Some fifteen miles on I come upon the town of Settle
Where I cross paths with some famous railway metal
I wind my way through the picturesque valley of Ribblesdale
Where once a planned reservoir bid did fail
Down to Nappa where my southerly flow turns more south-west
And with more magnificent scenery my banks are blest
So on to Paythorne where the king of fish does spawn
As the cool dank Autumnal days do dawn
I now pass close to the ruined Abbey at Sawley
Where my waters run deeper and more slowly
On to Clitheroe with its fine market and holed Castle
They say a reminder of some long passed hassle
To my left lies Pendleton and the mighty Pendle Hill
Where covens of witches their cauldrons did fill
With animal skin and bone, frogs legs and mashed up snail
A practice that could land them in Lancaster Jail
Between the villages of Great Mitton and Hurst Green
The confluence of the Hodder and Calder can be seen
At Dinckley I go under a bridge built on concrete blocks
And at Sale Wheel I cascade down over limestone rocks
I now pass close to the ruined Roman Fort called Bremetennacum
And I gain in strength as from the Calder the big Ribble
I have now become
I now meander my way down to the once serene Samlesbury
Where now thousands of people pass by in a big hurry
I now pass under the road bridge that had the half penny toll
And this is as far as my high tidal reaches of water do roll

Passing by the site of the finding of the Cuerdale hoard
And a road bridge that saw several bloody battles of the sword
The River Darwen joins me now and under the Old Tram Bridge I go
Passing by proud Preston's Parks where a ferryman once did row
Past the once bustling Albert Edward dock and the old Bull Nose
Where now only the idle rich on their pleasure boats do pose
Opposite Freckleton the 'Black' Douglas joins me
and salmon netters still ply
Passing Warton where high powered war planes reach for the sky
On my left bank lie the tidal marshes of Longton and Hesketh Bank
And high in priority for many wild birds they do rank
Now past lovely Lytham with its windmill and long lush green
And I ponder on the many fine ships on my waters it has seen
Now I see Banks and Southport and I feel my end is nigh
But as my sixty odd mile journey ends I can proudly sigh
For many forms of wildlife within my confines
I have nurtured and bred
Down through my green valleys on my long journey from Ribblehead
As I pass the sand dunes of St Anne's my flow is no more
As into the green, salty and rough Irish Sea I go.

Joseph Williams

The Seasons Are Always Changing

Bringing rain. Bringing shine.
Always with Your love divine.
Seeds are sowing. Soon will be growing.
Yielding grain which multiply.

Fish swimming in the sea.
Some are caught. Some set free.
The men who catch, and those who feed.
All blessed with Your love.

The land so fair, dressed in
glorious green when fine.
Autumn brings the gold and brown,
crunching leaves underfoot, the dew and frost.
Winter with perhaps some snow,
cold fingers and toes.
Long walks, wrapped up warm.
We look forward to the days of spring,
with daffodils and tulips.
Lambs springing through warm air.

Knowing You are always there.
To guide, to manifest Your love.
We only have to ask for advice.
When we are tossed upon the sea of life.
The strength will come as we swim for
the shore amidst the storm.

As we walk through the rain.
Your spirit will bring calm again.
The sun shine. The earth rejoice.

The choice is ours to follow You to the end
of the earth and beyond the moon and stars.

We are set free by the risen Lord.
He restores all faith, comforts those who pray.
May we always stay safe in the light of His love,
shining through eternity.

Every creature born will eat from His great bounty,
because He has sent the wind, the rain and sun,
to make it so.
The seasons are always changing.
Thank You Lord that You changest not.

Brenda Russell

Roy Remembered

We never talked, you and me,
Not like other people do;
Well, I would talk, and you would nod,
Whatever it was, we knew.

We never talked, you and me,
As you no longer spoke;
But with a nudge, a wink, a grin,
We often shared a joke.

We never talked, you and me,
And, really, that's a shame;
And yet we shared some times of fun,
And enjoyed them just the same.

We never talked, you and me,
But now you're in God's care,
Go talk with Him about His flowers,
He'll have a lovely garden there.

Brian Hartley

Carer's Lament

Oh Jo!
Why did you go
Down to the park
When you knew it was dark?
Got up in the night
And started a fight?
Peed on the mat
And blamed the cat?
They said you were mad.
I thought it was sad
That you went round the bend
Before you got to the end.

    Patricia Bowe

They're Going Shopping

Sitting at the window, I watch the world go by
Mums in tracksuits, pushing buggies loaded down with bottles and
                                                                         huggies.
   Going shopping.

I see old folks and young ones, some in between.
The cars racing past like a revolving screen.
I hear someone shout, Mum's lost her cool, thinks, that her toddler has
                                                                          made her a fool
Whilst she's shopping.

Short-haired, long-haired, bald as can be, tracksuits, jeans, sun tops
                                                                      and skirts.
Young girls passing each side of the road, rude stares, rude words
                                                                     sometimes smirks.
Each day I sit and see the same, young and old each playing a game.
The game is called life and isn't it right that we each must do it, every
                                                                  day, every night.

Tracksuits and trainers early till eleven, the girls' faces covered in
                                                                     Boots No.7.
They come out in posh skirts and short dresses,
They walk in crowds not one's/two's or three's, all dressed up like the
                                                                  honest bees knees!
After a bevy, a dance and cuddle they all walk back in a quaint merry
                                                                     muddle.

I sit at the window and watch again, seeing mums in anoraks plod
                                                               through the rain.
Babies in buggies, toddlers a splashing, mums shout to each other,
'Weren't last night smashing.'
They don't see me, their lives are so busy,
(they're going shopping.)

Buggies and wheelchairs electronically run.
Pass by my window daily for hours.

Makes me feel I should be out there too
That life is the same for them, me and you.
A woman, a baby in a buggy or a pram, being pushed by someone,
    she's gonna call Mam.
Then she's a schoolgirl with a uniform and a bag, calling all over
    twenties 'a miserable old hag.'
Then along on a boogie night she meets her fate, finding out she's
    pregnant far too late.

I sit in the window watching young and old, the young in their
    buggies wrapped up from the cold.
I see Dad with his son, Dad striding out, little boy on the run
Back from shopping.

April Treddle

Thinking

Am I looking too far and also too deep?
Am I trying to run before I creep?
I feel that there is something within my mind
Bursting the seams with words of all kinds
But I find it is like the will o' the wisp
Just floats away and leaves a fine mist.
I feel as though I am grasping into thin air,
I sit and think with a silent prayer.
So much crammed into a tiny space
To get it all out becomes a race.
As life goes on the time gets short
Memory gets dimmer so one is caught
In betwixt and in between,
A dilemma born or so it would seem.
All of a sudden a chink appears,
The mist has lifted, my mind has cleared:
Maybe I am not as old as I thought
My confidence back the words are brought
Out into the open to tease and taper
First finding a pen then on to the paper.

Dorothy Knight

Shattered Dreams

Oh dreams forlorn, where are you now
Dost thou not see the sweat upon my brow
The dreams I cherished, so long ago
When I first met my darling beau,
They held such love those dreams of mine
But they forgot with passage of time
They could be broken just like mine.

Around life's bend I'd failed to see
What cruel fate held in store for me
The Beau I did love so then
Became an ogre in its den
And oh how I do loathe him now,
He caused the sweat upon my brow
And as I lay me down to sleep
I dream of dreams, I could not keep.

Dorothy Morris-Hague

Another Space

Looking down far out in space, high black
Towers with secrets hidden.
Leave this gentle quiet place, leave your
Whispers here and go . . .

Ponder over rocky crag, don't dismiss how life
Came to its end.
Here amongst the shadows, peel off the
Memories of woe.

Tell me stories of life and death, of long
Ago and tribes long gone
Down the plateau amid the caves, a
History of time undone.

Take me hence and show the grandeur,
Of their cities which are empty now
Devoid of life and left to dust, lest they
Return and message give ~

Take me there and show me how, bring
Life to emptiness, light to dark
See it is there in distance far, a light
Comes forth and daylight dawns.

It unfolds a place of beauty, with spires so
High that gleams in sunlight bright and new,
And watch it glisten as with dew.

Susie J Burnette

Life

Every season has its reason, we laugh we cry, but
who knows why. To morning fair the night must
yield, while man must plough his chosen field.
Children grow and learn to know the compass is moved
By strife and creates a circle we call life.

Elizabeth Spencer

The Nursery School Teacher

The smile that banished morning moans
At being dragged there by our bigger siblings
Whose constant 'Be quick!' lashed like angry groans
Around our willing but still naive legs.

She kept a pile of knickers, underpants,
For small children lacking weeing control
And worse; a pile of clean rags for infants
With runny noses, to avert the sniffles.

'What shall we play today? Roy,
Will you try to catch us all, blindfolded?'
'Miss! I can do it!' one eager small boy
Offers head willingly to the scarf.

We did lessons after a little sleep
On canvas beds. Cosy, refreshed, avid,
Sitting around her in friendly heap,
We listened, we laughed, we learnt happiness.

Joan Kelly

Prophet Mohammed
('570-632AD Master of the Art of Love)

This world has seen many Masters of Arts before
But she has not seen the one who was a real Master
He was the Master of the Art of Love
He was the Father of the Art of Love.

He said love cares
He said love shares
He said love nurtures
He said love nourishes.

He said love builds
He said love trusts
He said love is always responsible
He said love is never irresponsible.

He said love holds families together
He said love holds nations together
Love builds bonds of Trust
Love builds bonds of Friendship.

He said love is meek
He said love is humble
He said love always forgives and never gives up: she perseveres
He said love always has a clean slate, no record of wrongs here.

He said love hopes
He said love has a heart
Her heart is so big that the whole universe would fit in
But there will still be room for more Flags and more Faiths.

Love always forgives
Love cherishes Life
Love sustains Life
Love is Life and hatred is Death: Let us Love God and Fellow
                                                                      Creatures.

Amen!

Haji Masud Ahmed

The Silent Army

Silently standing in long serried ranks
They have no need of weapons or tanks,
To create confusion and mild despair
In the hearts of all who see them there.

Silently standing in red and white
They have no need to move or fight
Sometimes we wonder why they are there,
But to move them away, no-one would dare.

Silently standing way into the distance,
They wouldn't offer any resistance,
Some get knocked over and lie where they fall.
Nobody goes to their aid at all.

Silently standing for hour after hour
Not doing anything, yet wielding such power.
Causing delays and moans and groans
This Silent Army of Motorway Cones.

Jean Wood

Strange Encounter

Walking down a country lane
Not a soul we passed
The wind was howling through the trees
Night was falling fast.

Suddenly we turned a bend
And right before our eyes
A tiny cottage came in view
A blessing in disguise.

We gave a knock upon the door
And heard a voice within
'Who are you, what do you want?'
We asked could we come in.

A lady bade us welcome
And said that we could stay
She gave us shelter through the night
Then waved us on our way.

On reaching home we found a map
To see where we had been
The country lane, the cottage
Were nowhere to be seen.

Suddenly we realised
Had we gone back in time
Things like that don't happen now
In this world full of crime.

What a sad reflection
On how things used to be
If we could just turn back the clock
To a world that's trouble free.

Edith M Stott

Michael's Poem

My eyes grow dim with tenderness awhile
Thinking I see you smile
And in the whispering trees so tall
Thinking I hear you call

You found the strength to call to me
Oh mom, my dearest mom
Then slipped away so quietly
That early morning dawn

Now you are long, long gone from me
Your face, your voice a memory
My son I'll miss you 'till I die
When our souls unite in heaven on high

Joan Latham-Trotzko

The Searching Eye

The searching eye
That pleads with mine,
That penetrates my heart ~
How can I not respond in love
To such a piercing dart.

'All I ask is a warm bed,
Simple food will do.
A gentle touch and a daily walk,
That's all I ask from you.'

The wistful look,
The searching eye
That penetrates my heart ~
The bond is made,
Our lives are joined,
Today, you'll have a new start!

Joan Thompson

St Crispin's Day
(In commemoration of Agincourt ~ 25th October 1415)

That rainswept month in distance past
When Englishman thought perhaps their last
In France's fields the time had flown
As they marched along to a fate unknown

From Harfleur's siege these soldiers now sought
Quick journey to Calais, and not be caught
Once safe in fortress Calais this band
Would turn their thoughts to Old England

But lying in wait stood proud Constable bold
With men at arms forty thousand fold
At Agincourt arrayed and not concealed
Stood France mighty power to England revealed

Great Henry the Fifth with his war-like hands
Placed on Brave England such stern demands
'The day's not dawned,' preached fierce King
'When France shall defeat, over England bring

'This morn must we make no mistake
So drive in soil, stout wooden stake
Then draw on long bow and fire so true
Those arrows,' called Harry, to his loyal few

That victory expected by assembled French
Would England's archers so bloodily wrench
Six thousand thin numbered English souls
Who on St Crispin's tore great gaping holes

This mass of arms by Dauphine raised
Was by shafts of arrows quick soon erased
By England's King great warrior son
The Dauphine's retainers were made to run

Then onward to Calais that part of England
Urged proud Harry the Fifth of our old land
To ship then home, where to loved ones say
'I was there with Harry, on St Crispin's day.'

    Brian Acton

Autumn Leaves

The autumn leaves are falling
Some of them are brown
And some of them are golden
Just like our monarch's crown
They fall just by the hedges
And right along our lane
Just see if you can catch one
They're falling just like rain.
Although I love to see them
I feel a sadness too
Because so long a time will pass
Before new leaves peep through
That won't be for ages
When May comes in with beauty
Days are bright and winter gone
The sun comes back on duty
To warm our lives so cold and chill
We now can 'cast a clout'
And see the skies all blue again
It makes us want to shout
Hooray! Those leaves are back again
The trees are cheering too,
So beautiful in full attire.
They're happy just like you.

Ethel M Crowther

Winter's Approach

September nights darken early now,
And ripened fruit is falling.
Friends gather at the autumn show,
Warm summer days recalling.

October's golden glow is fading.
Leaves change from green to darker hue,
The farmer tends the final baling,
Skies turn grey where once were blue.

November and the bonfire blazes.
Children rosy in the firelight glare,
Steamy breath on window glazes,
With morning fog on frosty air.

December now and much more jolly.
Windows gay and coloured lights ablaze,
Anticipation of the festive frolic,
The Christ child's birthday soon to celebrate.

Peggy Norton

Flowers Of The Wilderness

Our Last Wilderness is the loveliest place
Where peace and solitude mark the hours
Here are whispering streams and windswept fells
With birdsong at dawn and the glow of wild flowers
The silver-pink grasses, the blushing wild rose
On riverbank and beneath the trees
Each flower has chosen its own special place
Faces turned to the sun, heads a'dance on the breeze.
All the colours of the spectrum, daisies, poppies, hawk weeds sway
The Pyrenean lily, curled and gold, breathes a scent to take one's
                                                    breath away.
Magic names of magic flowers, columbine, heartsease, alcanet.
Too many to recall by name, but far too lovely to forget.
Examine closely one small bloom ~ delicate, detailed, perfect pure.
No human hand could reproduce such a masterpiece in miniature.
Mere words can never justice do, mere mortals barely understand
As they stop and gaze enchanted, at this wild and unspoiled
                                                    beauteous land.

Edna W Mills
The Slaggyford Poet

The Same Sky

My eyes gently rest, on a coastline unreal.
As far as I can see, rocks jagged, shiny and dark.
Washed over by endless waves, only to depart.
A turquoise sea laps over pebbles and sand ~
glistening and golden, a shimmering band.

All this is new and breathtaking to me ~ bright
sunshine, tanning, warming my face.
As I realise 'Lord' it's the same sky wherever I
might be.
A shining silver bird, brought me safely through
the air; away from the wind and the rain.

For a little while let me bask in a different
domain.
Tropical palms move, as they catch the breeze.
Thick rustic trunks, crowned with blades of green
shiny leaves.
Edging a walkway of parched yellow stone.

Such balmy days in bright winter sunshine.
As I look onto the distant terrain, I see mist-
capped mountains touching the sky.
Yes, 'Lord', the same sky wherever I might be.
Covering the universe for You to oversee.

Jean Jackson

The Dreamer

A dream should never be allowed to die
For then that dream has gone
And would be lost forever
Because the dreamer could not live on
And wouldn't that be a pity
Another dream lost again
So we should never let the dreamer die
Until that dream is real.

Abilgail E Jones

Venus

Venus is greater than the planet Mars,
She is now the queen of the morning stars.
I look at her, in the dark blue sky,
These are the words that I thought she'd reply:

'I am the queen of the morning light,
I'm also the planet of which people write.
Because you are a tiny child,
I'll shine at you, just soft and mild.'

Nicola Avino (13)

The Market Hall

Desolate and sad,
Why do I feel so bad?
My legs like lead,
I would sooner be in bed.

Responding to my inner hunger,
Into the Market Hall I wander.
Seduced by smells of coffee and cake,
Some hope of relief I begin to take.

From my balcony seat I can see
A colourful crowd just beneath me.
Crying children dragging their feet;
Exasperated mothers facing defeat.

Buying and selling,
The scene is compelling.
Everyone dancing to the tune of trade
And nobody caring where it was made.

Lovers walking hand in hand;
A cheerful, giggling adolescent band.
Senior citizens shuffling their feet,
Glad to talk to the old friends they meet.

This Market of cast iron elegance,
Has lured me back into the dance.
My journey now with lightened steps I take,
Thanking God for life and coffee and cake.

Gordon Harper

Compact

Hold my hand . . . don't let go
Take me where you want to go
A rush of blood the silence said
Memories instil inside my head
Hanging from the chain of life
Upside . . . outside and inside
Moisturise . . . feel soft within
Rub your body against my skin
Hold me close . . . feel the action
Hug and kiss the chain reaction
Stay with me for time will tell
Love is true as heads will swell!
Hold my hand . . . let fingers clasp
Hold me close within your grasp
Coiled springs beneath my soul
With only one place left to go
A see-through ball displays the middle
Words imply the Irish riddle
Labels hang to prove such cost
My heart and head . . . emotions lost
Mouth wide open . . . eyes intact
Exchange of power . . . love interact
Wrapped up in you the choice was mine
Love is true as love is blind!

Dean Urquhart

Not For Him

Not for Him a white speeding ambulance to a warm hospital ward,
only a slow donkey, to a cold cattle shed.
Not for Him a soft blue sheeted adorned cot,
only a prickly straw-filled animal's manger.
Not for Him a fleecy blue sleeping suit,
only plain, rough, swaddling bands.
Not for Him a team of doctors and nurses in watchful attendance,
only adoring, simple, shepherds from the Bethlehem fells.
Not for Him a cute teddy bear from Grandma,
only a new-born lamb from an unknown country lad.
Not for Him silver baptismal gifts from family and friends,
only frankincense, myrrh, and gold from ancient sages.
Not for Him an upwardly mobile carer in computers,
only a rapid descent into obscurity.

Not for Him a Security Four van to Strangeways,
only a laborious, burdened, uphill walk to Calvary.
Not for Him the anonymity of Her Majesty's prison,
only the shame of a public Roman Crucifixion.
Not for Him a quick, painless, release,
only the horror of a long lingering death.
Not for Him the hope of a reprieve,
only a mob-incited, unjust, conviction.
Not for Him a forgotten grave in Palestine,
But recognition as death's conqueror;
as our resurrected Saviour: the eternal King of heaven.

Brenda Gill

Loving Children

The children dance a little,
In grace and boldness, come yonder in dress,
Under a midnight moon,
Sparkling like a trillion stars in June.

When e'er we see the invisible presence,
Nature spirits appear in mirth and tidings
Bringing a million joys of hope across the briar,
Singing quietly in multitudes.

Today we remember laughter through the white portal,
Holding thoughts kindly from above,
Jotting down the wondrous rhyme,
Amazing flowers blow below windswept trees.

Where loving children sing sedately;
Where dreamy children bring their stories,
Sayings of love are read aloud, in comfort,
Where silence is golden and silvery.

So remarkable, so e'erlasting, so joyful and right,
Pictures of heaven, painting panoramic silver stars,
Shining to dazzle meadows fragrancy,
Linking the mind so victoriously.

Lost in great fields of yellow wheat,
Just playing hide and seek, unblemished,
Where the white clouds descend lowly,
Invaluable are all the children's hearts.

Where white and pink blossoms scatter in the wind,
Preoccupied with tender love, and giving,
Utopia's paradise crowns the rich purple heather,
Anew with magical blessings in plentiful array.

Lie a million dandelions, where fairies play unnoticed,
Where magpies dance their wings and plume.

James S Cameron

Fled Is That Music

Done, all is over, the scroll of poems rolled.
Idle seem the ideals
Which honeyed my grey heaven.
Kisses all made of air
They were laid upon chained veins
Now they must regain their origin beyond.

Go, all ringing rhymes
Delicious, singing rhythms of remembrance
All delighting dreams.

For we must part
Until the day the Gods will gladden
Where we shall be ever together
For lovely reason of art.

Follow, all words, you worthy sons
That being blessed this day must go;
Away, charmed chant, a carolling dance of maids
You too reclaim the cloud ~ bound realm.
Pegasus in fields of earth
Must fly through other meadows
Seek still with eyes of flame
The light of the smaller sun.

Jason Redvers Latham

If Only I Could Fly

How I wish I was you little sparrow
Over the rooftops I'd fly
And survey this world like you do
Without a critical eye
To watch the streams flow gently
Blissfully without any cares
Nestle in green velvet treetops
Fears I'd be unaware
To soar in the blue of the heavens
To see land peaceful and still
Fly where my wings would take me
Travel this world at will
If only I was a sparrow
There's nowhere I could not see
But alas I can only watch you
Take off in the blue from your tree

    Winifred Wardle

Neither A Duck Or A Swan

I wasn't a beautiful swan.
I wasn't an ugly duck.
You can forget what Hans Christian Anderson said.
Or what he wrote inside his book.
The real story of the tale is.
My mummy laid an egg.
She accidentally missed the nest she made.
Because she only had one leg.
The egg floated down the river.
Then it was picked up by a stray.
He took it to another nest.
Where his wife was about to lay.
The eggs hatched a few weeks later.
I was the first one to be born.
All the other ducks were eating bread.
But I was eating corn.
I had different colour feathers.
And a different shape of beak.
I could not speak their language.
To them, I was a freak.
One day my father said to me.
Quack, quack, quack, quack, quack, quack.
I couldn't understand a word he said.
I just jumped up on his back.
He took me up the river.
To a farmer's chicken pen.
I looked at all the birds around.
Then realised. I'm a hen.

Stephen Hibbeler

Flying

Drifting
Floating
Surfacing the sky
Leaving behind matchbox houses
Office buildings
A patchwork quilt of greenland
Interspersed with microscopic roads

Altitudes rising
Transparent clouds
Reflective like water
Transform into billowing clouds
Angels wings
Metamorphosing to snow

New angles as the plane dips
Diagonal sky marked with lines
Produced by other flights
Previous planes

Glimpsing a glowering sun
Dazzled by blinding light
Thirty thousand feet
From here to the ground

Cinsia Wilde

Autumn Glory

Autumn brings
crocuses to
bloom. Blanket of
leaves, scarlet
and bright. Gentle
breeze, tipped with
a scent delight.

Alan Hattersley

E Tenebris Lux
(Out Of Darkness Light)

What of the valley now the mines have gone?
What of the people who have to carry on?
Gone are the head stocks, the chimneys and the tips
Gone are the railroads, the wagons and the skips.

Deep underground, the silent caverns stand
But though the rocks by man's determined hand
Highways and byways down which the coal was brought
Destined for furnace, for homestead and for port.

Down in the darkness, there is no day or night
Never again the smallest spark of light
Never more a footfall, or a spoken word
Where once was noise and bustle, there's nothing to be heard.

Left as an underworld, that none shall see again
Sealed like a tomb forever to remain
A subject of legend and ailing memory
Part of our folklore to be, eventually.

What of men who laboured in the mine?
As they grow old their stories will decline
Tales of disasters of strikes and honest toil
Now all replaced by natural gas and oil.

Janet Cavill

Time Is Precious

Like a butterfly landing,
In a moment it's gone.
Life was so beautiful
When you came along.
Time was the enemy,
Love came to an end.
Time was the healer.
Time is my friend.
Allusive yet precious,
As precious as gold.
The magic of future
As yet to unfold.
I'll love you forever
It won't be the same,
But beauty can come
In so many ways.
When I see the sky
As blue as can be,
I'll be thinking of
You, and know you'd
Be thinking of me.

M Rossi

Beauty ~ Louise

Questioning, trusting gaze,
    from wide-spread eyes,
Parted, ready lips,
The slight inclination of the head,
    held away in calm tension,
From the narrow relaxed shoulders.

The pale, drawn face
    with its well-defined cheekbones
And the lace-edged cuffs,
    slightly drawn back
From slender wrists, tapering down
To the tiny hands laid delicately
    within the folding material.

Pettr Manson-Herrod

Autumn Signs

When the summer's day grows old
And you feel that hint of cold
Signs of autumn are in the air
Now things are changing everywhere.

Leaves are falling from the trees
Carried away by the autumn breeze
Flowers give their last fair bloom
Autumn is here winter soon.

Across a grey cold autumn sky
To distant lands the birds will fly
Where was green has now turned brown
Wearing autumn's golden gown.

Woodland creatures think of sleep
Digging holes that go down deep
They gather food to store away
To wake upon a fine spring day.

Linda Bellamy

Heart Strings

You are not my children
Siblings to prise apart
You have your own lives to lead
Your bed to lie in
Made or unmade
Your fight is not mine
Nor mine, the task of referee
I can merely watch you
As you struggle like flies
Caught in the spiders' web
Not knowing that
The web is old
And the spider; long gone.

Alan Gale

A Moment For Life

A year of grey days are worth it;
For a moment like this.
A moment in which
I laugh so hard;
That I cry.
A moment when I hear a voice,
At the end of a telephone line
And immediately I smile.
A moment in which
I can share;
My joy,
My fears,
My woes.
A moment in which
I know;
I'm Home.
A moment spent;
In the company of true friends.

Rachel C Zaino

My Italian Hat

It sits there in silence, saying so much
The woven straw pattern, I get up and touch
It's stuffed full of memories, of good happy times
Of Italy's music and scented pines
The people are happy, friendly and warm
We follow the moon, along beaches till dawn
The traffic it halts, for its old folk to talk
Not noticing they chatter, and then they walk
Nobody bothers, time has slowed down
In the small villages, away from the town
The sun bakes the stones, in sandy walls
Someone is singing, someone else calls
Across from Sorrento, Dasuviouse bubbles.
Awakening from sleep, to give out more troubles
Pompeii's people are suspended in time
In clay, and potash, and sand, and lime.
Just a short boat ride, you land on Capri
You won't have time, to see all that's to see
The grotto's blue waters, all shaded to black
To see all it's splendour, you'll have to come back
So you lift the straw carefully, because you know that!
All of these memories are stuffed in that hat.

Sandra Oates

The Swan

With grace and serenity she glided through the madness.
Her soft whiteness cut a swathe through muddied water,
She witnessed much in her effortless cruising,
Her soft down a sanctuary from the savagery.
She had seen the malevolence of youth,
The intimidation of the lead weight,
Her elegant neck the target for a vindictive oar.
Was it always like this?

Head bent and shoulders hunched,
Barrier against driving rain
A slight drink induced stumble,
It was easy for the swan to keep pace.
The swan saw them before the stooped man,
Drug-filled youths intent on destruction,
Property or person, it matters not.
And still the swan glided through the madness.
She heard the shouts, the laughter, the screams, the splash.
And as the battered body floated by her,
Was it always like this?

Began the day blue and bright,
Paddling expertly through debris and madness,
Witnessing the lifelessness of the bruised and mottled body
Hauled unceremoniously onto the sodden bank
Surrounded by men in blue, far too busy
To notice her serenity and elegance.
She sailed beyond the fuss, picking her way expertly
Through debris and madness.
Will it always be like this?

A Jones

Game Of Chance

You've got the probability of a coin.
50:50.

Not the same.
Different for one,
Exact for another.
That's you. But why?

I have no idea what I've done.

He used to be gentle and kind.
Almost angelic . . .
Now his horns are growing.

She used to be happy, very contented.
She loved the way he was.
Now all she wants is to cry.
Maybe even to die . . .

Flip the coin.
Which side will it land on?

Heads.
You're beautiful, outgoing and pure.
I'm in love, sure and positive.

Tails.
You're evil, hurtful and hateful.
I'm thrown into confusion.

I have no idea what I've done.

But then again, it's only a game.
Who knows what it's going to land on next?

  Candice Buchanan

Mother Nature

When nature seethes with anger,
Oh my what have we done,
Did we really upset her for the
Sake of having fun?
The seasonable winds are reeling,
Rockets to the ceiling.
The ozone layer, nearly bare.
Are we without a care?
I'm no philosopher, you tell me,
What is in space out there?
Who's got the answer?
Who's got the key?

D Williams

Ode To The Braying Donkeys

List woman, still the braying donkeys
    Fools, they had their day.
Woman what aimless sloth possessed thee
    What thoughtless manner, why
Didst thou take that man, a stranger yet today?

Tied in wedlock to a questioning heart
    To an eye opened wide that questioned the heart
To an ear ere closed to all but the ass
    Woman, they questioning heart still beats, alas.

The gifts of wit and tongue were thine
    The gift of wisdom mine
For the richest prize I'd change this not
    Mine stood the test of time.

List woman, the braying donkeys stilled
    Behold the ghost of ages past
Behold what might have been
    A scattered kin, an aching heart
Damns a troth that should have been.

John Morrison

The Good Old Days

Go down to Swan Street then in through the foyer
It is like going back in time
You can sense the ones who where here before
Anticipation as you stand in the line

The posters covering the walls around
Of names that were big in their day
Now part of the nostalgia
You pass them and go on your way

The stage where so many greats have trod
As they ascended the ladder of fame
I don't think fortunes were the same in their day
But fame has always been fame

The stalls are all dressed in red and gold
What a beautiful sight to see
Imagine it in the Good Old Days
The audience decked out for a spree

The Circle Bar, a place of its own
You gaze back towards the door
Wondering whose ghost will follow you in
What memories of this place are in store

The Grandfather Clock in the corner
The old lighting that used to be gas
Casting shadows on the pictures and posters
That make eerie shapes as you pass

We who live in this city are fortunate
This gem is still here to be seen
The Leeds City Varieties
Of the Music Halls the queen.

Peggy Hunter

Have You Been There?

When you feel out of sorts and you just can't explain . . .
And it isn't an ache or yet even a pain . . .
But a great sense of loneliness deep down inside,
Tho' you may be surrounded by folk on each side.
This terrible emptiness disturbs your peace,
You long for a solace to make it all cease,
The darkness of night seems to offer a balm,
(Why in the gloom do the restless find calm?)
I've always found when I'm feeling 'quite low',
To walk 'neath the stars brings some soft inward glow,
No longer frightened but shielded, secure,
(If only this figment was made to endure!)
You wish that these hours could forever go on,
And never again feel the threat of the dawn,
For then life's adversity crowds all around,
Once again you have lost the sweet haven you found!
Was it a nearness to God and His care?
For He was the only one, who was with you there!

Catherine O'Neill

Untitled

As time goes on I tend to feel,
The world around is not quite real
A thought, a dream, a distant sound,
In one whole lifetime what have I found?
Is this for eternity or just a phase.
Will I awake in a sort of haze
And will the whole mystery unravel
As through the unknown mist I travel.
Somehow, I hope when I *do* awake
Life starts again as a new daybreak.
If I had the power to start anew,
With what time is left, to carry through
My vows, made now, to all mankind,
Would I awake, this time to find
That all through life there was no theme
The whole experience just a dream.
But wait, this surely can't be so
For what of God and the faith I know.

Nan Milton

My Memory

It happened late one evening
Or was it early dawn
Perhaps it was the afternoon
Or let me think was it mid morn
Anyway it was a Saturday
Oh no that isn't right
A Wednesday is when it was
Though Thursday seems to strike a light.

It really doesn't matter
As it happened long ago
The man knew all about it
He told the story blow by blow
In fact, it was a woman
Or was it just a lad
It might have been a schoolgirl
I must be going mad.

Whatever way the story was
It wasn't true to tell
And I can't recall what happened
So perhaps it's just as well.

Betty Park

Laura

Laura, Laura Paisley lass,
You left this world, far too fast,
Your mother weeps as you sleep,
And father, is praying for you to awake,
In the arms of angels, at St Peter's gates.

Laura, Laura Paisley lass,
Your little frame, was not to blame,
Evil followed you, that fair night,
It pulled and dragged you, from God's light,
As you fought, for your little life.

Laura, Laura Paisley lass,
Twenty-two roses bloom for you,
As white doves fly overhead,
Taking you under their wings,
Setting your soul free from evilness.

Laura, Laura Paisley lass,
Brother is crying from his heart,
Staring evil in the face,
Wishing hanging, would take place,
For justice, and peace of mind.

Laura, Laura Paisley lass,
The town hall clock rings for you,
St Mary's says mass for you,
People of Paisley, say farewell,
To the Paisley lass that went too fast.

H Muir

The Old House

'Tis only a memory now that it's gone,
Where once stood the old house,
There's a bungalow and lawn,
The old cottage garden with sweet-scented rose,
The honeysuckle, lavender, the vegetables in rows.

The seat in the corner where one sat at ease,
Watching the fluttering of butterflies, the bees,
The cosiness, warmth and friendship inside,
Peaceful, loving, with a great inner pride,
Independent, content, no grandeur was sought.

But the old folks grew ill and their old house was bought,
Sadly they've gone leaving a starkness in place,
Now there's nothing to show,
But a modern new race.

Annie McKimmie

The Rain
(Helensburgh Bus Stop)

We grumble about the rain
As it puddles at our feet
Pouring from the heavens
Sometimes turns to sleet

Battling with the elements
Wind lends rain a hand
Umbrellas turn outside in
We can hardly stand

Patiently at the bus stop
Cold, wet, hands clenching
Dancing cars quickly pass
Water jets are drenching

Home at last eventually
Firelight by the telly
Scenes of famine, drought and dying
No rain for years, not any

Give us rain the pouring rain
Dry parched countries pray
Their existence threatened
As they long for rain each day

I'll have rain where the grass is green
Crops in abundance grow
Thankful to have our seasons
Though the rain might turn to snow.

Mary Hudson

Hope

The angels are coming to take me away
I've lived my life or so they say
To shed a tear ain't that bad
Although some say it would be sad
To drift back in time may ease the pain
It's either that or go insane
The windows of light reflect in your eyes
For after all, you have said your goodbyes
It's strange to think that there is no tomorrow
Only time! ~ and a little sorrow
You think of your family and time gone by
And it's only natural to give a sigh
Then hope appears in a very strange way
Maybe just maybe it will keep the angel at bay

William D Watt

Brigadoon

One small windmill at which I must tilt
Is the cult of the Celt in the kilt:
Haggis, tartan and sporrans,
Recitations of Burns,
Fractured vowels that make Englishmen wilt.

They're all kin to Macbeth, Thane of Cawdor,
Bonny fighters, first class cannon fodder,
Wee, uncouth, hairy men
Living down in the glen
Like their archetype, Sir Harry Lauder.

Norman Bissett

Scotland My Home

Scotland my home
The land of my birth
Such scenic beauty
The pride of my soul

The grandeur of mountains
Whose peaks are of snow
With streams raging down
As if meeting a foe

Burns and streams
So clear and so bright
To the lochs they do journey
By day and by night

These dark still waters
Are beautiful to see
Surrounded by forest and mountain
And a life that is free

Oh beautiful Scotland
You will always be
Land of my birth
And home to me.

Hazel Smith

Bonnie Dundee

I was born in nineteen and twenty-nine,
    In the 'City Of Dundee',
Where my Mother had her ninth child,
    And the Baby Girl, was me.

Visitors, always love this City,
    And they all, agree,
That we have the best, of both worlds,
    Living near the hills, and Sea.

It has a lovely, City Square,
    Where local people meet,
To admire, the beautiful fountains,
    As they occupy, a seat.

And if they climb, the Law Hill,
    To view, the River Tay,
They'll see down, to Broughty Castle,
    And also, Invergowrie Bay.

There's Glorious flowers, in all the parks,
    Or if they prefer, the beach,
Broughty Ferry, is only three miles away,
    So well within, their reach.

It's never ever, crossed my mind,
    To ever leave, Dundee,
'Cos I've spent over seventy-one years here,
    So it will 'aye be dear, to me.'

    Jean Hendrie

The Home Help's Holy Grail

The home help's Holy Grail,
Is her trusty mop and pail,
Whilst she does this morning's dusting,
For the Chippendales she's lusting,
The sight of dirt is so disgusting,
Now the TV aerial needs adjusting,
She's been cleaning here at no. 10,
Since only she and God knows when,
A bon Viveur of good taste,
She fills the sandwiches with meat paste,
'Take your time luv' more speed less haste,
Then it's off to tip the waste,
How can such an honourable maiden remain so pure, so chaste?
'I'll have to go and wash the old lady's face',
'Then vacuum the new rug just in case',
'Then mend them ole curtains made of lace',
Everything's spick and span and in it's right place,
Then a pause for tea at half-past eleven,
Truly the meek shall inherit heaven,
A chocolate biccy,
'I've put on two pound doesn't it make you sicky!'
Then it's home to make the old man's meal,
Then in an armchair she'll congeal;
Then again it's up at seven,
For there's nothing so demeaning,
AS to start the spring cleaning,
And so this home help stars her daily travail,
Truly the home help's Holy Grail,
Is her trusty mop and pail,
So I write this verse to the countless Mrs Mops,
Who dust the china, empty out the slops,
And visit countless butcher shops,
And be one of life's good neighbours,
So now I'm rattling a few sabres,
For Mrs Mop at her labours.

Alan Pow

Kitty

He lays all his cards out on the table,
Growls at me and spits out,
'OK tiger, why don't you put your money where your mouth is?'
He gets my back up
Yet, I rise to the challenge.

After beating me at several cat and mouse games
I realise, just how tame I look
And, how easy it was for him to get his claws in.
Purring back at me with that Cheshire cat grin
I know, there's not a whisker of a chance I'll escape

Because the fat cat always gets the cream.

Lynsey Calderwood

McLeod In The Clouds

Farewell, Sandra, this is goodbye
You're away to a job where you work and fly
Leaving your friends in Barrhead Sanitaryware
For a new career that's up in the air

You will look sexy in uniform and hat
By the way, I was paid to say that
Serving meals and pouring teas
Above the clouds and over the seas

You will have to know your job and politely speak
Like 'Welcome aboard, I'll show you your seat'
And not 'Park your arse, I'll get you a drink
Right where's the booze? Now let me think'

So listen, pal, you take care
Whilst you're working up in the air
And when you come to see us from over the sea
Don't forget the duty free

Wear your uniform when you pay us a visit
So we can look and say 'Who is it?'
You will succeed 'cos you're not dim
So it's good luck from me and good luck from him

John Carrey

Eternal Youth

Some say life begins at forty.
Not according to Janice next door.
Her back gave out
Her teeth played up
She felt all ragged and wore.

She started a youth club
For Eddleston's teens
In an effort to relive her past.
It was a hit from the start
And for the most part
Is a Monday night hoot,
What a blast!

She really is a jolly good stick
And a garrulous party animal.
Her teeth are now fine
And her back all in line.
Thanks to youth club
Echinacea and wine.

So, when you hit forty
Don't go all warty
And give in to age and its ails.
Get down the youth clubs
Forget about *your* subs
Ask Janice
For further details.

Kathleen Dow

A Day

A day at work
Petty triumphs
Like speaking down the phone
And being
Understood.

No thinking allowed
In brackets private.
Thoughts are stilled.
The photocopy machine
Takes care of that.

Time is elastic
Taut on Sunday
Dragging Monday on.
Mondays are mice
Scampering on the heels of
Heavy Sunday lunch.

Close your mind off.
It is only Monday.
Count the hours to go.
Only forty, then you're free.
It's like death
With a happy ending.

Gillian Hare-Scott

Sunshine

When someone gave me sunshine
It was another boost to my pride
On the long road to recovery
From life on the darker side
To you, probably just a token
To me much more than that
A testament to faith in words well spoken

Denis M Rae

Big Issue

He stands at shops and corners
'Big Issue' he is selling
The people pass and say 'No thanks'
tears in his eyes are welling

He's just a lad of eighteen years
a homeless youth at that
he's sleeping rough, and that I fear
will be upon some mat

So come on folks what's a measly pound
the book is good to read
It's full of news and this one pound
will help these lads in need

Rodger Boyd

Before The Concrete

I twist and turn my head at the tenement window
to try and glimpse the distant sky
and wish that I could dwell among the clouds
so that through the heavens I could fly.

But as I tread so wearily round this town
and feel far below my tired feet
another world from long ago and far away
a green land now lost in eternal sleep.

I once had heard that Glasgow was a forest
ringed by many a shimmering lake water
the jewel of the West was that valley
and the Clyde its shining daughter.

If I could journey far back in time
this one thing I would earnestly pray
to lie beside those ancient lakes
even if it were only for one day.

In quiet contentment my eyes would look
at that peaceful, verdant idyllic scene
my very soul at rest by the great forest
so knowingly ancient and sublimely serene.

As with silent feet the wind walks out
across the dark gleaming lakes
and white swans bow their stately heads
as snowy plumes it softly, gently shakes.

The hills and dales roll eternally on
into a dim and unremembered distant past
and rearing up forbidding the forest whispers,
'I am archaic. Forever I shall last.'

But then with time an ugly forest of concrete
a titan horror started to grow and rise
in a land that once knew and blessed
Holy and Majestic Clutha's dear paradise.

And so again I turn and twist my head
but see only the monstrous pain
and a dead, thick weeping sky
pouring out its soul numbing rain.

   John Bonnar

from: Nursery Rhymes

There was a broken man
he had a broken wife

they had been living
for too long

on the edge
of a broken knife.

Jonathan Claxton

Castletown Carol

When the grass was pale and silvery.
Shimmering through each December.
Crimson leaves floating in the sky.
How could I forget to remember.

Does the snow lie on Penshaw monument?
Can you still see it glittering bright?
let's all wish a merry Christmas to Castletown tonight.
Angels sing their sweetest songs from the stars over Castletown
                                                                               tonight.

Does the cauld lad still roam the ruins
By silent stones where the gargoyles frown?
Are the bonny young golden boys
Still swallowed by the mine ~ going down ~ going down?

Do the children play in the liney
And fish the Wear from Barons' Quay?
Its blue water flows through the wind and the rain.
Please can I come back again?
Please can I come back again?

Let's all wish a merry Christmas to Castletown tonight.
angels sing their sweetest songs from the stars over Castletown
                                                                               tonight.

Elizabeth Stephens

Pie Crust and Pot Noodle

Aa, that's me
Running in from school
Cloth cap and jumper and heavy football boots
I've made a pie crust our Joe!
I'll remember it always . . .

But I'm 70 today
Didn't think I'd make it!
Turning, slowly from the window
There's Dolly, dozing in the chair
We've just had our Ruby

And yes, that's the grand-bairns playing in the lane
4 BMXs and designer footwear
Robots discarded on the step
Cardboard box for a ramp
I used to play with a hoop

A Pot Noodle's to die for! shouts Josh from the kitchen
We've got a talking tree Grandad
Says Merry Christmas and everything
That's nice son
We had a paper garland hanging from the light

I look at Dolly, wondering
Will we make our Diamond?
And there, through the window is Da
Drinking, on his own at the end of the bar
Aa, dreaming of that pie crust . . .

Val Stephenson

What Is The Meaning Of Life?

I am sitting here, wondering,
Why?
Life is just tormenting

Life is a never-ending circle,
That finally comes to an end.
Why?

Life is a piece of paper you treasure,
Then finally throw away,
Only to discover you do need it after all.
Why?

We just take life for granted,
Until it's too late.
Why?

Life is like a stage,
Until the curtain falls.
Why?

Life is like a bar of chocolate
Savour the taste,
'Cos when the last bit's gone,
It's the end.
Why?

When people are laughing,
And enjoying life,
Join them.

Don't let the curtain fall on an empty stage.

Kathryn Kaupa (16)

The Fog On The Tyne

The fog on the Tyne is all that's left, the river looks so sad.
Things really couldn't get much worse, the situation's bad.
No more the churning of the foam, as tugs and ships steam by.
There's just a steady ripple, brings a tear to the eye.
The South to North-Shields ferry even on those gloomy nights.
Won't need to sound her hooter or use her traffic lights.
There's a clear view of river both to starboard and to port.
Why can't we just reverse the years now there's a pleasant thought.
When ships were lying four abreast on both sides of the river.
The sight of these majestic hulks would set your hearts a-quiver.
When one thumbed through the 'Shields Gazette' for sailings in and out.
Would take up two whole columns, and that's without a doubt.
Looking know across the Tyne, quiet and serene.
Where once was so much bustle, it now seems just a *dream*.

Norman H McGlasham
South Shields

Ladies Of The Skies

Do you believe in angels
The loving ladies of the heavenly skies
For they look down upon us
With their bright and beautiful hazel brown
Emerald green and sparkling angel blue eyes

They look after your body
They look after your soul
They look after everyone
Be they young or old

They walk by your side
Throughout your young and old lifetime
And try if they can to keep you
Out of lots of pain and sorrow
Because every loving and caring angel
From up in heaven above
Is someone's loving and caring mother
Down here on earth below

Donald John Tye

Dream Catcher

On a hot sticky day in the middle of June
I took time off to visit the moon
When I arrived, surprise what I saw
A broken old house so I knocked on the door
In just a moment it opened wide
I slowly walked forward and stepped inside
Before me a shadow declared, 'Who are you?'

'I'm the landlord and your rent is due!'

'Are you really the owner of this barren land?'

'I own the hallowed ground upon which you stand.'

'But I have nothing, not a penny to my name
Not even a memory from whence I came.'

'An innocent heart is all that I ask
Keep a pure soul that is your task.'

With these few words the ageing light
Turned into darkness and day became night
A strange sort of story this may seem
But anything is possible by the power of your dream

Barry Cuda

Paper

Two pieces of paper represent a life.
No words of love or passion,
no mention of a wife.
No records of the moments
of the love that filled our hearts,
of the years that passed like seconds,
or the pain when forced apart.
Two bits of paper.
One marked birth the other death
indicate that we were here,
but don't record a life of love,
or pain or fear.
Not much to leave for many years
of wishes, hopes, and sometimes tears.
A life ~ two bits of paper.

Walter Christmas

A Thought For Winter

The winter time is long and hard.
No warming sun; no singing bird;
No hint of summer days to come.
So shrouded in the rain and gloom
The blood runs cold, empty the eye,
Heavy the heart and deep the sigh.
Yet, if the soul can once recall
The slender willows by the fall.
The river path where thrusting trees
Were softly green. While on the breeze
The scent of clover, and the sound
Of lilting birdsong all around.
There in the orchard bright the glow
Of cherry blossom on the bough.
Remember golden gorse that grew
Upon the hill where I and you
Climbed hand in hand, and then looked down
Across the spread of field and town.
The world enchanted our domain
Where only Gods and lovers reign.
A place once seen thro' lovers eyes
Becomes alike to paradise.
Let winter come and have its day,
Quite soon its wrath will die away.
Whilst in my heart will ever be
A summertime of memory.

Vivian Finlay

The Key

Where has it gone ~ the magical key?
They've searched and searched for ~ the magical key
Peered and probed for ~ the magical key
Hoping it exists ~ the magical key
Enigma without ~ the magical key
I know it exists ~ the magical key
Please discover ~ the magical key
My only escape ~ the magical key
Mind locked without ~ the magical key
Who will recognise ~ the essential Me!

Kathleen Potter